Hov

101 Tips, 1

Charlotte Moyer

Receive my next book for free!
Exclusive promotions, updates and newsletters
Join my Book Club Now

Table of Contents

WELCOME

Firstly I'd like to thank you and congratulate you for downloading "How to Bake Perfectly: 101 Tips, Tricks and Cheats for Baking Recipes".

Inside this book are a variety of baking suggestions that will transform your baking. Not only will you impress your guests with your improved skills but also stun them with delightful flavors and presentation. So dust off your baking utensils and take advantage of these neat tips, tricks and cheats.

It's time to bake our way to food heaven!

Thank you

Charlotte Moyer

PS...Don't forget to join my Book Club

INTRODUCTION

If you are looking for a new experience in the kitchen, then baking can be just what you need. Imagine the pure joy of biting into freshly made bread that has been out of the oven for less than an hour. In addition to tasting delightful, it is a wonderful way to make your home smell wonderful as well. It will also really impress your family and friends. After you have mastered the 101 tips, tricks and cheats in this book, you will easily be able to master any recipe that you see.

As you read through this book, you will find tips that will help you save time. Furthermore, you will find tips to cut down the time that you have to spend in the kitchen. You will have the advantage of knowing that you are feeding your family with foods that are not filled with preservatives. These preservatives have been tied to many diseases including cancer, yet world governments continue to let them be used. The great news is that learning to perfect your baking skills by adopting the easy tips in this book, you will no longer be feeding your family with baked goods that contain questionable ingredients, but with wholesome food that will give you peace of mind.

Researchers also know that baking is a great way to increase your personal happiness level. You will boost your confidence level as you master each new skill. None of these skills require any special equipment or hard to find supplies. Instead, they rely on supplies you probably already have on hand.

You will also find tricks that will allow you to make fewer mistakes in your baking. These tips, tricks and cheats have been developed over the course of a lifetime by a person who loves to cook. Instead of taking the rough road, making mistakes and having to learn from them, you will quickly master the art of baking breads, pies, tarts, cookies, cakes, cupcakes and more.

As you start following the easy to understand advice in this book, you will discover that you quickly improve your skills. You will learn secrets that will help you bake bread that is not too dense and make cookies that do not burn. Additionally, you will learn to present food in innovative ways that not only look great, but are easy and efficient to do.

No one likes to spend a large amount of time in the kitchen. Everyone is very busy. If you have been putting off learning to bake, because you think you do not have the time, then stop procrastinating and get busy now. You owe it to yourself to learn something new. Even if you have been baking for years, within the pages of this book, you will learn new tricks that will transform your baking from boring to exciting.

When you follow the cheats in this book, you will find that your time in the kitchen is probably much less than it already is, and you will enjoy a new level of baking confidence that you have never felt before.

This book contains no recipes. Instead, it shows you how to take your favorite recipes and improve them using tips, tricks and cheats that make them taste better than ever before.

Now without any further ado, let's start baking!

Chapter 1: Bread

The first bread probably dates back at least 30,000 years when water and a cereal grain were accidentally combined to make a flat bread. By the time, that the Greeks had risen to be world leaders, they had discovered leavening and knew many different types of bread. The Romans were not far behind where a piece of stale bread was used as a disposable plate. After the meal, the bread was then given to the poor or a dog. Do not worry. When you follow these easy bread tips, stale bread will never be a problem at your house again.

Tips, Tricks & Cheats

1. While it may be tempting to simply stick the flour cup into the flour sack and fill it with flour, do not do this as you will get too much flour. Instead, use a spoon to fill the measuring cup. Do not tap the cup to see if you can get more flour to fit in. Simply level the top with a flat edge. Using too much flour, means that your bread will not rise properly.

2. If your recipe calls for flour or all-purpose flour, substitute this with bread flour when baking bread. Bread flour is higher in protein so this helps the bread to rise higher. Additionally, using bread flour ensures that your bread does not come out rubbery. In order to make this substitution, simply use the same quantity amount. It will not change the taste of the bread, but your bread will look much nicer.

3. If your bread seems to be getting brown too fast in the oven, do not turn down the oven temperature. Instead, carefully remove the bread from the oven and cover it with an aluminum foil tent. In order to build the tent, simply fold a piece of foil in the middle to resemble a pup tent. Then, fasten the edges to the side of the pan. This will stop your bread from getting too brown, while your bread finishes baking.

4. If you are baking a yeast bread, and suddenly need to stop mid-way, then simply put it in the refrigerator after the first kneed. You can leave it there for up to 24 hours. In fact, this

slow fermentation technique allows the carbohydrates to convert to carbon dioxide completely. Just make sure to let the bread return to room temperature before you continue with the recipe. Additionally, the bread may bake faster, so be sure to keep an eye on it.

5. If you want a crisp crust on your bread, then you will need two shelves in the oven. Put one rack as close to the bottom of the oven as possible, and the other near the middle. Fill a pie pan with water and set it on the bottom shelf. Then, put your bread on the middle shelf. As the water evaporates, it will cause your bread's crust to become crispier. Watch the water level and refill if needed.

6. If you are using fruit in your bread, then mix the fruit with a little flour first. Otherwise, your dough can become a gooey mess. Just put the fruit into a large mixing bowl, and add a little flour from your recipe. Then, toss the fruit until it is well coated.

7. If your recipe calls for punching down your dough, then fold it instead. In order to fold the bread, take it out of the bowl and place it on a well-floured surface. Flatten the dough just slightly and gently score it into three equal parts. Fold the two outside parts on top of the middle part. Following this technique, increases the bread's surface tension, so you will end up with a much more beautiful loaf of bread.

8. While your bread will smell wonderful straight out of the oven, do not cut into it immediately. Instead, wait at least 15 minutes. Then, cut with a serrated knife. Waiting not only makes the bread easier to cut, but for about 15 minutes after coming out of the oven, it is still cooking. Cut into it too early, and you can cause the bread to fall, as you are disturbing the air pockets within the loaf.

9. If it is time for your bread to rise, but you are in a hurry, then sit in on a heating pad. Turn the heating pad on low and be sure to cover the bread with a damp towel. The heat from the heating pad will cause your bread to rise faster than normal without causing any damage to the bread.

10. If you want to know if you have kneaded your bread enough, break off a very small piece. Roll it into a ball, and then try to stretch it out. If it does not break easily, then it has been kneaded enough. In fact, you should see it become translucent before it tears. This is called the gluten window. If it tears easily, then you need to knead it some more.

11. The water that you use can make a huge difference in how well your bread rises. If you have water that is treated with chlorine, it is important to treat the water, because the chlorine can interfere with the rising process. Additionally, hard water causes the bread to have less volume. Soft water causes the yeast to be more active. In order to eliminate all these problems, simply boil your water first and then let it return to room temperature.

CHAPTER 2: CAKES

Archeologists have found the earliest known cakes in the remains of Neolithic villages. They were probably made from just crushed grain and cooked on a hot stone. By the time that Romans had risen to power, cakes had become much more sophisticated and were often used as an offering to gods. It was not, however, until the 18th century that eggs replaced yeast in most cake recipes. You will want to have plenty of eggs on hand so that you can make many wonderful cakes when you follow these tips, tricks, and cheats.

TIPS, TRICKS & CHEATS

12. It is essential to bake your cake in the middle of the oven. Cooking it too close to the top causes the top to brown too quickly, while cooking it too close to the bottom causes the bottom to brown too fast. Additionally, if you are baking more than one cake, make sure to leave as much room as possible between the pans to ensure proper air flow.

13. If you want a lighter cake, like an Angel Food cake, make sure to use cake flour. Since it has less protein, your cake will turn out lighter. Alternatively, if you want a more tender cake that may be a bit denser, then use all-purpose flour. Do not use bread flour as it has too much protein and your cake will be very dense.

14. If you need to slice a cake layer in half, then first insert toothpicks every inch around the cake at the level where you want to cut it. Then, hold two ends of dental floss tightly on the ends and pull it through the cake. Carefully lift the top half off the bottom supporting the cake as much as possible.

15. Never put a just baked cake on a flat surface where air cannot get under the cake. Instead, allow the cake to rest in the pan for 20 minutes on a wire rack covered with a damp towel. Setting a hot cake on a flat surface where air cannot get under the bottom will cause the cake to get soggy.

16. Additionally, use a spatula to loosen the edges of the cake from the pan before inverting it to ensure that it comes smoothly out of the pan. The damp towel will encourage the cake to slip out of the pan more easily.

17. Unless stated, most recipes assume you are going to bake the cake in a silver colored pan. If you are using a dark colored pan instead, lower the oven temperature by 25 degrees from what the recipe calls for to ensure proper baking.

18. In addition, oven temperatures can vary widely, so make sure to use an oven thermometer for best results.

19. Never use a bigger or smaller pan than the recipe calls for, because the cake will not raise properly.

20. It is essential that you use room temperature ingredients when making a cake. If you need to warm up your ingredients in a hurry, then stick the butter in the microwave for a few seconds. Put eggs in a bowl of warm water and let them sit for 10 minutes.

21. If you are putting your cake on a glass plate, then dust the plate with powdered sugar first. The sugar will keep the cake from sticking to the plate. Additionally, the cake will stay moist longer. You can even lay a paper doily on the plate before you dust it to achieve very pretty presentation.

22. If you want your favorite cake recipe to rise a little higher, simply add a tablespoon of meringue powder to the mix. Meringue powder can be found in almost all grocery stores, often where decorative cake supplies are kept. Do not mistake meringue powder with cream of tartar. Meringue powder contains gum, egg whites and powdered egg whites.

23. When making butter cakes, in order to keep it from sticking to the pan, combine equal amounts of shortening, oil and flour. Spread evenly over the pan. The best way to apply it is to use a pastry brush. If you make too much, the mixture will keep for several weeks in the refrigerator. Just make sure to let it return to room temperature before using.

24. You need to rotate the pans while baking a cake, but not until the batter has set thoroughly. Therefore, make sure to wait until two-thirds of the time has elapsed. Then, gently rotate the cake. If you are baking cakes on multiple racks in your oven, then move the top cakes to the bottom and the bottom cakes to the top to ensure that your cakes bake evenly.

25. Cakes require fresh ingredients so that leavening happens properly. If you are afraid that your baking powder is too old, then put a tablespoon of it in a cup of water. You should instantly see bubbles.

26. While almost all flour will keep at least four months, it is a great idea to sit the original bag inside a plastic bag to ensure that it does not attract weevils.

27. If a recipe requires oil but you find that the cake comes out oily, simply substitute this with the butter. Melt slightly beforehand using the same weight in butter. Viola, more oily cakes.

CHAPTER 3: COOKIES AND BISCUITS

The history of cookies probably traces back to ancient Iran, then called Persia, about 700 A.D. when the first sugar was cultivated. Archeologist believe that the first cookies were actually prepared as test cakes. Regardless of whether you call them cookies, biscuits, keks, biscotti, or koekie, following these hints will allow you to bake perfect ones each time.

TIPS, TRICKS & CHEATS

29. Choose your fats carefully when making cookies. If the recipe calls for margarine, then avoid margarines that contain 80 percent or more vegetable oil. These oils do not combine well with the other ingredients. Therefore, you will end up with tough cookies. They also do not brown well. The best butter to use for baking is unsalted butter. If you open the refrigerator and all you have is salted butter, then simply reduce the salt in the recipe just slightly.

30. In recipes where you need to cream together the butter and the sugar, do not be tempted to rush this step. This step usually takes about 10 minutes. Butter and sugar are not properly creamed until they are double in volume. Make sure to scrape the butter and sugar off the sides of the bowl on a regular basis.

31. Make sure to check the expiration date on all your ingredients. If your recipe calls for baking soda and you are unsure how fresh it is, then combine a little with vinegar. If it is fresh, it will bubble instantly. If not, then toss it out and buy some fresh.

32. Additionally, if you are using nuts, then make sure to smell them. Nuts can turn rancid quickly. When they do, you will smell a horrible smell.

33. Most cookie recipes taste best when you allow the dough to chill. You can choose to let them sit for only a couple of hours, but for best results, let them sit in the refrigerator overnight. This allows all the flavors to blend. The cookie dough will also be firmer and

easier to work with than dough that has not been chilled.

34. If you are baking multiple batches of cookies, then make sure that you have enough cookie sheets. Never bake cookies on a hot cookie sheet. Doing so will cause the dough to melt. When dough melts, it affects the cookie's taste and texture. In addition, make sure to keep the dough away from the heat of the oven.

35. Be very careful not to overmix your cookies. If you do, then your cookies will turn out tough. Instead, make sure to read the recipe very carefully and stir only when told. Usually it is enough to simply stir the dry ingredients together and then stir in the wet, but make sure to check the recipe.

36. If, once baked, your cookies stick to the pan, then return the cookies to a warm oven for about one minute. Then, immediately remove the cookies from the sheet with a thin spatula. Always cool your cookies on a wire cooling rack to avoid soggy cookies. Remove the cookies to the wire rack just as soon as you can.

37. Pay attention to what size eggs the recipe calls for and use the right size. In the United States, a large egg contains four tablespoons, while a medium egg only contains three tablespoons. Therefore, for every four eggs in a recipe, you will need an extra egg if using medium. If the recipe does not specify, then it generally is a good idea to use extra-large eggs.

38. When you bake cookies use two cookie sheets, one on top of the other. Most cookies will perfectly brown using this method, but if you want your cookies a bit browner, then remove the bottom cookie sheet and let them bake for another minute. As always, make sure to use an oven thermometer to make sure that your oven is at the right temperature.

39. If you are making rolled cookies, then be careful how much flour you put on your rolling surface. The dough will absorb the extra flour and come out tough. Additionally, this can cause the edges to brown too quickly. If you have trouble with this, then skip the flour all together by rolling your cookies between two sheets of wax paper.

40. Always divide your dough into at least three batches, only removing each batch from the refrigerator when you are ready to work with it.

41. If you love the taste of fresh baked cookies, but do not always have time to start from scratch, then consider making some dough ahead of time and freezing it. For chunky cookies, like oatmeal raisin and chocolate chip, divide the dough into individual cookies before freezing them in a plastic bag. If you are making slice and bake cookies, like shortbread, roll the dough into a log and freeze the whole log. If you want to freeze cut-out cookies, like sugar cookies, then roll the dough into a pie crust shape and freeze flat.

42. If you like to make wheat breads, but find that they always come out dense, then try a no knead recipe. While the rise time will be longer, these breads usually come out less dense. The microwave can be the perfect place to let the bread rise, but make sure that no one

turns it on while the bread is inside.

43. Measure the liquid in your dough very carefully. A dough can almost never be overhydrated, but it can certainly be under-hydrated. Therefore, the next time you try the recipe, up the amount of liquid slightly. It sometimes helps to let the bread rest about 10 minutes between mixing the bread and kneading it.

Chapter 4: Pies & Tarts

Pies and tarts share many similarities. Yet, there are some definite differences. First, pies have sloped sides, while tarts have straight sides. The goal with a pie crust is to make it flakey, while the goal with a tart crust is to make it firm and crumbly. Regardless of whether you are making a pie or tart, follow these essential hints to ensure a huge success that will leave your family and friends crying for more.

Tips, Tricks & Cheats

44. Tarts have only a bottom crust. This crust is usually moister than a pie crust. In order to make the tart crust, it is vital to use the right flour mixture. The baker should combine an equal amount of all-purpose flour and cake flour. This creates a firm crumbly crust for the tart.

45. Place the pie or tart pan on a baking sheet between putting it in the oven. This will help keep the crust from becoming soggy. If you are making a fruit pie or tart, then melt some jelly in a pan on the stovetop and brush the inside of the crust. This will give the crust extra flavor and further keep it from becoming soggy.

46. It is important to choose the right thickener when making a pie or tart. If you are using apples, then use all-purpose flour to thicken the apples. If you are using fruits that are acidic like cherries, plums, lemons or peaches, then thicken the fruit with tapioca. If you are making a dairy tart, then use cornstarch.

47. The colder you keep the pie crust dough, the more likely it is to keep its shape. Therefore, make sure to chill it again after you roll it out and before you bake it for best results.

48. If you have trouble getting your pie or tart crust done, then bake it in the bottom third of your oven. If you choose to do this, however, keep a special eye on the crust. If it browns to quickly, cover it with a layer of aluminum foil or use a special tool designed just for this

purpose.

49. If your fruit seems to disappear in your tart or pie, try prebaking the fruit first. If you like soft fruit, then slice the fruit and put it in a bowl. Bring a pan of water to a boil and pour over the fruit. Let it sit for 10 minutes and then continue to prepare as usual. If you like softer fruit in your pie or tart, then put them in a heated Dutch oven and cook them on the stove for 10 minutes.

50. If you are using nuts in your pie or tart, then line the shell with a layer of nuts. Carefully lean a nut along the edge of the shell. This helps to make sure that the taste is spread evenly through the pie or tart. The oil from the nut also helps keep the crust flakey.

51. The filling of a pie or tart does not set firm until it has been removed from the oven, so make sure to let the pie or tart cool before trying to cut it to ensure that you do not have a runny filling. If you find that the fruit is still running, then you can return it to a preheated oven for up to 10 minutes. Of course, you will need to let it cool again.

52. Be careful not to overcook your pies or tarts. If you can stick a knife in it, and it easily comes out, then it is done. The middle will usually still be jiggly. Overbaking pies and tarts causes them to become lumpy.

53. Do not open the door while the pie is cooking as it will let in a blast of cold air. Instead, wait until the pie should be almost done to check on it.

54. Combining high pectin fruit with low pectin fruit helps the filling cook better. High-pectin fruits include apples and blueberries. Putting just a little in a low-pectin pie or tart yields better results that taste delicious. Popular low-pectin fruits include blueberries, cherries and strawberries.

55. The amount of water that you need to add to your crust depends on many different factors. Therefore, it is important to not add to much water at one time. Start with one-fourth teaspoon and continue to add water a drop at a time until the dough will make a sticky ball. You should never need more than one-half teaspoon.

Chapter 5: Cupcakes

Compared to many foods, cupcakes are a relatively new creation. Historians believe cupcakes were invented in the United States during the 19th century, although numerous legends exist about exactly where. Many of the first cupcakes were called numbers because the batter contained one cup butter, two cups sugar, three cups flour, four eggs, 1 cup milk and 1 teaspoon soda. Regardless of what ingredients you are including in your cupcakes, follow these tips, tricks and cheats to make them efficiently.

Tips, Tricks & Cheats

56. Make sure to use a cupcake pan when baking cupcakes. The best pans are dark colored. They are also very heavy. You need to start with a perfectly clean pan. After filling the liners, make sure to clean off any drips. These drips will burn while the cupcakes are cooking and can cause problems if they spread and come in contact with your cupcakes.

57. The best cupcakes are made with the very best ingredients. If you are short on cash, then concentrate on buying the very best vanilla. You will find real vanilla and vanilla extract. While the extract will be noticeably cheaper, you will be able to taste the difference. If you are making chocolate cake from scratch, then you should also buy quality chocolate. Most fair-trade cocoas are wonderful for cakes.

58. Pay attention to how long you are to mix the ingredients. The reason that this is so important is that the more you mix the cake, the more air you are removing from the batter. When the air is not present, your cupcakes will not raise as high. Overmixing causes long tunnels in your cake that can blow the top off your cake. On the other hand, if you do not mix enough, then the gluten will not develop correctly. Therefore, the cake will often sink in the middle and crumble easier. If the recipe does not specify, then mix until the ingredients are just combined.

59. It is vital that you use a cookie scoop to ensure that all your cupcakes are exactly the right size. Overfilling some cups and under-filling others means that they will not cook evenly. The easiest way to make sure that you have exactly the same amount of batter in each cup

is to use a large cookie scoop for regular size cupcakes and a small cookie scoop for small cupcakes.

60. If you are not able to frost the cupcakes immediately, then wrap each cupcake in plastic wrap to ensure that they do not dry out. In addition, either put them in an airtight container or freeze them as soon as they are cool. This will keep them from drying out which is one of the main reasons that people claim they do not like cupcakes.

61. Making cupcakes is exciting, but you really need to leave the oven door shut while the cupcakes are baking. Opening the oven door, lets cold air into the oven and disturbs the cake's structure. In particular, you are breaking down the gluten and fat structure, so you will end up with a fallen cake that is extremely dense. You should only open the door one time while the cupcakes are baking. When the cupcakes are two-thirds done, open the door one time and rotate the pans. If you are baking on two shelves, also move the bottom pans to the top shelf and vice versa.

62. Make sure to bake your cupcakes right after you have mixed the batter. While you are mixing the cupcakes, you have forced air into the batter so that they will bake properly. If you let the batter sit, this air will go back into the environment. Then, your cupcakes will not be moist, so make sure to bake them immediately.

63. In order to get the most air into your cupcakes, always mix by hand. If you really want to use a mixer, then never turn it above low speed. This encourages the air to go into your batter, so that your cupcakes will be moist. Additionally, doing this will help your cupcakes not fall or rise so high that they split. Choosing to mix your cupcakes by hand, also means that you have less dishes to wash.

64. Liners are essential for making great cupcakes regardless of the type of pan that you are using. When buying liners, look for liners that are greaseproof. While they can sometimes be hard to find, they will look nicer when you are done. The reason is that the grease fades the color, so using greaseproof liners traps the grease and leaves the wrapper's colors alone.

65. When you are putting your ingredients together, you need to start and end with the dry ingredients. Add the wet ingredients in the middle. This helps to trap the air in the batter and helps to form the gluten that the cupcakes needs to bake properly.

66. As soon as your cupcakes come out of the oven, tip them gently on their sides, so that air can circulate under their bottoms. As soon as possible, move the cupcakes to a wire rack to completely cool. As soon as the cupcake is completely cool, add frosting, because it will help to trap the moisture. Since cupcakes are small, they can lose moisture quickly, becoming dry.

67. Cupcakes taste best on the day that they are baked. If you need to transport frosted cupcakes, then you may want to buy special boxes to transport your cupcakes. Alternatively, you can turn the cooled and washed cupcake tray upside down and cover it with aluminum foil. Push the foil gently down on the bottom of the tray. Take your time so

that you do not tear the aluminum foil. Turn the tray over and wrap the edges of the foil over to the right side to hold it tight and make it look great. Turn the cupcake sheet back over and insert the cupcakes into the holes that you have created. You can either choose to carry the tray this way or insert it into a box.

Chapter 6: Pastry

If you love pastry, then you can thank the Romans. The first pastry was invented to be wrapped around meat to help keep it from drying out. By the 17th century, people in the United Kingdom were making many different types of pastries. If you have always had trouble making perfect pastries, then follow these tips, tricks and cheats.

Tips, Tricks & Cheats

68. It really is up to you whether you'd prefer to use lard or butter. Lard crusts are easier to work with than butter crusts. Therefore, if you are a new pie baker, consider using lard in your crust. Alternatively, butter crusts are harder to work with, but the result will be tastier. The choice is up to you.

69. When you are combining the lard or butter and the flour, the more you cut in the shortening, the flakier your crust will be. While you can stop when there are no pieces left larger than a pea, for really flaky pie crusts, keep working until it resembles bread crumbs. Do not use a food processor for this step. Instead, use a pastry cutter, as you will have more control of getting the pie crust to just the right consistency to roll.

70. While you want to let ingredients come to room temperature to successfully bake most things that is not the case when you are making pie crust. Instead, concentrate on keeping your ingredients as cold as possible. This includes the flour. Refrigerate the dough for a few minutes between each step to ensure that the ingredients stay cold. The ingredients and the dough should stay below 60 degrees at all times.

71. Make the crust at least two inches bigger than the diameter of your pie plate. This ensures you have plenty of crust to cover the pan well. The extra can always be trimmed off.

72. Many people find it hard and time consuming to crimp a pie crust. Instead of taking a half-hour to complete this step, using a strand of round beads instead. Simply lay the beads around the outside of the shell, and push the beads down gently. Using this technique, you will have a crimped pie crust in under a minute. Once crimped, gently pull the beads off the crust and bake as usual.

73. It is easy to make your pie a golden brown. Simply combine a little egg yolk with very little water and brush it on the pie crust. Then, every few minutes, brush the crust again. You will discover that brushing the pie multiple times will make it look prettier when done. If the outside edges begin to get too brown, cut a circle from aluminum foil. Then, cut out the middle just slightly smaller than your pie shell. Use it to wrap the rim as it will stay in place better than strips of aluminum foil. When putting the foil in place, make sure to remove it from the oven and shut the door so that you preserve your oven temperature.

74. If you have trouble making flaky pie crusts, then substitute vodka for the water. Freeze the butter for about 20 minutes and use a cheese grater to grate the butter. Then, make sure that you work the butter in until you have no lumps larger than bread crumbs. While this

will take a little longer, you will be able to taste the difference in the finished product. Additionally, the pie crust will look much prettier.

75. As mentioned the best pie crusts are made with cold ingredients. Many recipes suggest putting an ice cube in the water to make it cold. Skip this step while speeding up the pie crust making process. Instead, put the amount of water that the recipe calls for in the freezer until a thin sheet of ice forms on top of the water. It will be the perfect temperature to use.

76. Many people find it difficult to add just the right amount of water while continuing to work the dough. In order to eliminate this problem, use a cruet. Before you try to roll your crust, sprinkle a few drops of water from the cruet on your work surface and then put your wax paper on top. The water will help hold the wax paper in place. When done, just pick up the wax paper, and turn it upside down over the pie pan. Then, drop the pie crust in place.

77. If you are going to prebake your pie crust, then take some precautions to make sure that it holds its shape. Start by covering the bottom with parchment paper. Then, put lima beans on top of the parchment paper. Your crust will stay stable and not bubble. Once the crust is baked, then simply throw away the lima beans and parchment paper. Continue preparing the pie as usual.

78. If you are making several different types of pastry and need to quickly tell them apart, then use a different decoration technique on each one. For example, during the 18th century, the edge of fruit pies were fluted, while sweet pies were left unadorned.

Chapter 7: Traybakes

There are many different types of traybakes. Common examples include flapjacks, blondies, brownies, and blondies. While in the United States, these are commonly called brownies and sheet cakes, in the United Kingdom, they are lumped together and called traybakes. Regardless, follow these tips, tricks and cheats to experience wonderful results.

Tips, Tricks & Cheats

79. You may have been taught that a toothpick inserted into the center of a traybake should come out clean, that is not the truth. If it comes out clean, you have already overbaked the traybake. Remove it from the oven immediately. When you insert a toothpick in a traybake, a few crumbs should come out with the toothpick. If you still see liquid on the toothpick, however, you will need to bake the traybake a few minutes longer.

80. If you are in a hurry, then start with a box or bag mix. Make sure that you buy a quality brand. Then, make it your own by adding ingredients to the basic mix. You can cut up chocolate candy and put in it or add marshmallows. You can crush peppermints and add them to the mix. There are so many things that you can do, that once you start being creative, you may never make the same traybake two times again. The choices are yours, and this is a great way to save time.

81. If you have trouble with the traybake not wanting to release from the pan, then put a towel in the kitchen sink and get it wet with extremely hot water. Wring the excess water out of the towel and lay it flat on a work surface. Set the traybake on the towel for about one minute and the traybake will release. Use a thin spatula and concentrate on getting under the traybake liftingit from the sheet. Try to put your serving plate and the baking sheet as close together as possible.

82. If you are frosting your traybake, then brush it first with a dry pastry brush. This will remove any crumbs. Then, you can frost the traybake as desired. If you do not do this, it is nearly impossible to keep the crumbs out of your frosting.

83. Cutting traybakes should be done with a damp serrated knife. It is a two-step process. Start by pushing just hard enough to cut through the crust at an angle. Then, cut through the traybake straight up and down. Stop and clean the knife between each cut with a damp towel making sure to leave the knife damp.

84. Choosing the right recipe to meet your tastes goes a long way to baking a traybake that you will love. When comparing similar recipes, if you like a more cake-like traybake, look for recipes that have more eggs. Alternately, if you like chewier traybake, then look for a traybake with multiple ingredients and fewer eggs. Finally, if you like a more fudgy texture, then look for a recipe with more butter and less flour.

85. If you have trouble with the bottom of your traybakes burning, then set the pan on a pizza stone or on another baking sheet. The addition of another layer will keep the bottoms from burning. If the edges seem to be cooking too fast, cover them with aluminum foil. You can also use a wet towel wrap around the outside of the pan to stop the edges from getting done too fast.

86. In order to keep traybakes from drying out, only cut the amount that you want to serve. Cutting them ahead of time encourages them to dry out. Make sure to cover any unused portion immediately. Most traybakes can be kept at room temperatures. Even putting those containing cream cheese in the refrigerator only extends their life one day.

87. Many people have trouble with traybakes humping. If you have this problem, then you can make a large X with a knife through the middle of the cake before baking. This disrupts the air bubbles and will usually keep the cake from humping. If you still experience problems, then make sure to use baking strips around the outside of the pan. Always make sure to level the batter before baking.

88. If you have trouble with the top of your traybake cracking, then the next time that you make the traybake, add a package of unflavored gelatin to the mixture. It will help the top stick together.

89. Using a different technique when putting together your traybake will often help add moisture to the finished product. Start by separating the eggs and beating the yolks until creamy. Then, add the sugar and beat until well combined. In a separate bowl, beat the egg whites until frothy. Then, add them to the sugar mixture stirring to combine well.

Chapter 8: Decoration and Presentation

There are many beautiful ways to decorate and present your sweets. Presentation can make your food look much more elegant. You can use many different techniques to decorate and make you baking enticing. The great news is that you may very well already have the supplies that you need at home.

Tips, Tricks & Cheats

90. Instead of using a plate to serve your sweet on, consider making a chocolate bowl. Simply melt some chocolate and pour it into a muffin tin. Let the chocolate cool just slightly. Then, set a balloon down in the melted chocolate. Let the chocolate cool completely and peel away the balloon. Now, dump your chocolate bowl out of the muffin tin.

91. Freeze a cake before you frost it. You can freeze the cake from a few hours up to a month. It does not matter. Then, frost the cake before it thaws. This creates a firmer surface and makes it easier to thaw.

92. Instead of just serving breadsticks on a plain plate, make an edible bread basket. Cover a large heat safe bowl turned upside down with strips of bread. Then, working from the other direction, weave more sticks through the original pieces. Push the strips together at each place that they meet. Then, braid two strips around the bottom. Bake the bowl until the bread is done and then gently remove the bowl. Fill as desired.

93. Lay a piece of parchment paper on top of a baking sheet. Arrange peppermint candies on the parchment paper in a design that is just a little larger than the traybake, cupcake or piece of cake that you plan on serving. You can use any design that you want. Put them in a preheated oven until they melt. Be careful when removing them, as they will be very hot.

94. Strawberries can easily be made into a decoration. Take a strawberry with the leaves still attached. Turn the strawberry so that the leaves are on the work surface. Cut four or five thin cuts almost all the way through the strawberry. Apply some gentle pressure to the strips, and they will fan out.

95. Flavor, flavor and more flavor. No matter how beautiful or enticing your presentation is concentrate on the flavor of all your baked goods. Nobody likes to be disappointed when the food doesn't live up to expectations.

96. Sanding cupcakes is easy and fun. Frost the cupcake as normal and then cover the frosting with edible sand. You can create a fun looking snowcone cupcake by putting the cupcake in a Styrofoam cup after it has been frosted and sanded. Do not forget to add a plastic spoon to compliment the look.

97. Make apple tarts the size of apples. Then, hollow out an apple and insert the tart into the apple. Serve with a fork. Guests will not only enjoy having a fun looking dessert, but you

will not have any dishes except the forks to wash making cleanup a snap.

98. Instead of using a regular top crust for a pie, cut the pie crust and form into long strips. Then, braid three of the strips together. Starting in the middle of the pie, wrap the braid around the top of the pie in a circular motion.

99. Cake pops are easy to make and taste so good. Just make your batter into a ball and insert a lollipop stick. Form the cake pops using a small cookie scoop. It is easier to frost cake pops if you freeze the pops first. Additionally, remember that it only takes a little bit of frosting to cover the cake pop. If you are making these for a special occasion, then frost the pop in a color that goes with your party theme. Place the finished pops in a block of Styrofoam.

100. Marzipan is a fun way to decorate almost any sweet. You can easily create almost any shape or mold that you desire. After shaping, place it on the top of the sweet.

101. Decorate the plate with the dessert already on it. Simply lay a piece of cake on a plate. Then, add a quick swirl of syrup to the plate and dessert. This not only makes an elegant presentation, but is extremely quick to do. You will find a variety of syrups made just for this purpose or you can use syrups made for ice cream.

Conclusion

Thank you for the opportunity to tell you about these tips, tricks and cheats. You are now ready to become an expert baker by applying the material found in this book. You are now prepared to make great tasting breads, pies, cakes, cookies, tarts, and so much more.

As you follow the tips, tricks and cheats contained within this book, you will probably discover that you love to bake. You will also find that you have a new love of your time spent in the kitchen, since you now know exactly what to do. You are also prepared to decorate and present your baked goods in innovative ways that make them beautiful.

As you begin to put the information in this book into practice, you will feel better because you are now able to bake with the full knowledge of the ingredients. You have learned the importance of using the best quality ingredients that you can find. You have also learned that except in the case of pies and tarts that it is vital to keep your ingredients at room temperature to successfully bake. Of course, you have also learned many tricks to help you do that more quickly such as putting eggs in a bowl of warm water. Furthermore, you have learned the importance of checking the oven temperature using a thermometer and to keep the oven door closed so that you do not ruin your baking with a blast of cold air. You have also learned the importance that mixing ingredients correctly to trap air in your products to give it the right texture. Of course, these are just a few of the many things that you have learned within the pages of this book. Now, the next step is up to you.

We also offer several other books so make sure to pick out a new one to read. Finally, if you would like to learn more about the joy of baking, then make sure to sign up for our newsletter.

Most importantly, however, have fun baking. There is absolutely nothing more fun. We know that you will most certainly indulge all of your baking delights.

HAPPY BAKING!

About the Author

I am a mother to three beautiful children and a wife to a wonderful husband. I have a passion to teach others and can often be found volunteering in my local community.

During college I worked within my family catering business to support myself. After graduating I opened a chain of small cafes that I ran successfully for a number of years. Now whilst being a stay at home mom, I am able share my skills, knowledge and experience through my books. I feel a great deal of satisfaction when helping others and seeing them flourish to their maximum potential.

Please check out my author page on Amazon to see my latest publications. Please don't forget to **join my Book Club** for free books, newsletters and updates.

Once again I want to thank you for reading my book. I really hope you got a lot out of it.

If you enjoyed this book I would really appreciate it if you could leave me a positive review on Amazon. You can **click here** to go directly to the book on Amazon and leave your review.

I love getting feedback from my readers and reviews on Amazon really do make a difference. I read all my reviews and would really appreciate your thoughts.

Thanks so much.

CHARLOTTE MOYER

Other Books By Author

How to Make Money from Home
7 Steps to Earn Money from Baking Recipes

Have you often been told that you have a flair for baking? Are you regularly praised for your rich, creamy cheesecake, complimented on your luscious lemon bars and exalted for your perfectly chewy, moist chocolate chip cookies? If so, then is time to monetize your passion and talent. This eBook is one that you definitely need to pick up! It will provide you with all the information you need to start baking yourself to a steady income. Whether you are just looking for some extra cash or want to ditch your job and work for yourself, baked goods could be your saving grace!

Printed in Great Britain
by Amazon.co.uk, Ltd.,
Marston Gate.